ELEVATING
Your Elevator Speech

by Dave Sherman

Elevating Your Elevator Speech

Copyright ©2005 by Dave Sherman

ISBN: 0-9742504-7-3

Edited by SageBrush Publications, Phoenix, Arizona
Interior Design by The Printed Page, Phoenix, Arizona
Cover Design by Ad Graphics

Printed in the United States

This book is dedicated to all of the Chamber of Commerce members that I have seen deliver terrible elevator speeches. If it wasn't for you, I never would have realized how badly this book was needed and I certainly wouldn't have worked so hard to help each and everyone of you find out what it takes to deliver that perfect 30 second commercial.

Contents

Dedication v

Please Read Before Starting This Book! xi

Section One 1

1st Flr.   An elevator speech is not a sales pitch. 3
2nd Flr.   You'll need more than one commercial. 5
3rd Flr.   Off the cuff rarely works. 7
4th Flr.   It's important to make them laugh.. 9
5th Flr.   The KISS method always works. 11
6th Flr.   Sometimes less is more. 13
7th Flr.   Dare to be different. 15
8th Flr.   No pen means no notes. 17
9th Flr.   Make sure you edit your comments. 18
10th Flr.   Your elevator speech can kill or create a relationship.. . . 20
11th Flr.   No reaction means an ineffective elevator speech. 22
12th Flr.   Job hunters need a great introduction, too. 24

Section Two 27

13th Flr.   Your typical opening just isn't cutting it. 29
14th Flr.   Only use words that everyone will understand. 31
15th Flr.   Leave the industry buzzwords within your industry. . . 33
16th Flr.   Do everything you can to make your name memorable. . 35
17th Flr.   A good prop always works. 37
18th Flr.   Pictures speak more than a thousand words. 39
19th Flr.   The price is not always right. 41
20th Flr.   Be careful of the 3Ms. 43
21st Flr.   Everyone offers good service. 45
22nd Flr.   Always remember your name. 47
23rd Flr.   It is not the length that counts. 49
24th Flr.   Mention your businesses one at a time. 51
25th Flr.   Beware of the SRQ. 53
26th Flr.   Let your business card provide the details.. 55
27th Flr.   People really only care about the benefits you offer. . . . 57
28th Flr.   Being different makes you more memorable. 59
29th Flr.   Don't bury the best parts. 61
30th Flr.   Always try to create mental pictures. 63
31st Flr.   Who a good client is for you is meaningless for us. . . . 65
32nd Flr.   Watch the number of acronyms you use.. 67
33rd Flr.   The most powerful word in elevator speeches. 69
34th Flr.   Always end on a high note. 72

Section Three **75**
35th Flr. How you say it makes all the difference. 77
36th Flr. Be careful of your verbal speed. 79
37th Flr. The simplest things are the easiest to forget. 81
38th Flr. Speak up and be heard. 83
39th Flr. Practice really does make perfect. 85
40th Flr. Overcome the number one fear of creating connections. . 87
41st Flr. Overcome a few more fears in your life. 89
42nd Flr. Always keep a smile on your face. 92
43rd Flr. Every good introduction starts with a good handshake. . 95
44th Flr. Remember to look them in the eye. 98
45th Flr. Speak Your Speech Before You Write your Speech. . . . 101

One to One Elevator Speech Consulting With Dave Sherman . . **103**

About the Author **105**

Order Form. **107**

Hi. My name is Dave Sherman. I want to thank you for taking a look in my book. When I came up with this title, I was under the impression that EVERYONE knew what an elevator speech was. As I researched my material, I soon discovered that not everyone was familiar with this term, so that's where I'd like to begin.

An elevator speech is a short (fifteen- to thirty-second, 150 word) sound bite that succinctly and memorably introduces you. It spotlights your uniqueness. It focuses on the benefits you provide. And it is delivered effortlessly.

Elevator speeches are intended to prepare you for very brief, chance encounters in an elevator. But elevator speeches are not just for elevators! You should use your speech whenever you want to introduce yourself to a new contact. That could be in the supermarket, waiting in line at an ATM, getting your morning latte, or sitting on a plane.

The reason a powerful elevator speech is so important is because the most well-known icebreaker of all time happens to be, "What do you do?" People never fully understand the great opportunity you have when others ask you this question. Unfortunately, most people just babble out the first thing that comes to their mind and then wonder why people don't seem intrigued or interested in what they do.

Think about how you normally answer a question like this. You might say your title and the name of your company, and then you'll typically ramble on with a series of random thoughts that will probably confuse, bore, and torment other people. The first thing you need to understand is that NO ONE REALLY CARES WHAT YOU DO FOR A LIVING!! Sorry for the abruptness of that statement, but it's the truth. Most people ask you about what you do because it's the only way they know to break the ice.

Now that you know what an elevator speech is, let's talk about why you need to be elevating yours. An elevator speech is meant to do four things:

- grab the attention of the listener
- engage them in conversation about your business
- identify the main benefit your company offers
- encourage people to say the three most beautiful words in the world—tell me more.

Does yours do this? If it doesn't, don't feel badly. Did you know that less than two percent of the people that I talked to have a well-crafted elevator speech that they can recite at a moment's notice? No one really thinks about the importance of an elevator speech until I explain to them the amount of new business they are missing by not having one.

Think about how frequently people ask you the question, "What do you do?" Let's assume that someone asks you that question every day of the working week. That would mean that you are asked this simple question approximately 265 times per year. That is 265 opportunities for you to create the beginning of a new connection and potentially start a new business relationship. How many of these 265 opportunities are you squandering because you don't have a great way to answer the question—what do you do? Well, this book can help you turn many of these opportunities into new business for yourself.

Now that you understand what an elevator speech can do for you, I suggest you take this book to the first available register, to the person standing behind this products table, or possibly even to me, and purchase this book so you can start to feel more confident, more comfortable, and more successful when people ask you what you do.

Please Read Before Starting This Book!

Before you dive into this book, allow me to provide you with a few explanations.

- Throughout this book, I refer to elevator speeches in many different ways. I sometimes refer to them as 30-second commercials. I often refer to them as personal introductions. You will never see me referring to them as a unique selling proposition; I've always hated that one. I use these different names because these are some of the different ways people describe an elevator speech.

- There are traditionally two places where somebody can deliver an elevator speech. Most of the time, you will deliver your elevator speech to people one at a time. This will happen at business functions, trade shows, networking organizations, and a multitude of other places.

  However, if you regularly attend organized networking functions, such as the ones put on by chambers of commerce and leads groups, you will have the opportunity to deliver your elevator speech in front of a group of people.

  This book will address every imaginable way to help you with your elevator speech, whether you do it one to one or in front of a large group. All of my tips will benefit you, regardless of how you deliver your powerful elevator speech.

- You will notice that at the end of many of the tips, there's a box titled Action Plan. These boxes are meant to encourage you to select a specific date that you will start using one of these tips. After reading each tip, if you feel that you would like to use this idea while developing your elevator speech, select a date, and write it in the little box. Also, make sure you fold down the corner of the page so you know where to find each of the tips you want to start using. When you have made use of each tip, unfold the page, and go on to the next one. When you have unfolded every page, you should have a well-crafted and powerful elevator speech that will make people stop and take notice.

Section One

An elevator speech is not a sales pitch.

Q. I've always heard that an elevator speech is not supposed to try and sell anything. It's just supposed to inform people. If that's the case, why is that so many of the thirty-second commercials I hear are a sales pitch for some product or service?

WHY, you ask? It's because people don't know any better. They never learned how to craft a great introduction, so they listen to what all the other people say and copy them. The problem is that most people stink at delivering a good elevator speech.

Without a doubt, one of the biggest mistakes people make is when they try to use their elevator speech to sell their product or service. The places where you hear the most elevator speeches are tradeshows, business functions, networking events, and so forth. These are not the proper environments to try to sell somebody your product or service.

Your goal when you deliver your introduction should be nothing more than to grab people's attention, engage them in a conversation about your business, and encourage them to ask for more information. You'll notice I said nothing about a sales pitch or trying to close the sale. You need to be able to create some sort of connection with the person before you try and go in for the kill. If your elevator speech is effective and people seem interested in what you are saying, ask for a card and call to set up an appointment with them to show them everything. This way, you will be t.-ter prepared and will know much more about the people with whom you are meeting.

Always remember, your elevator speech isn't meant to sell anything. It should be used to help you open a few doors and allow you the opportunity to walk right in.

✔**Action Plan:**

From this day forth, I will make sure my elevator speech will be informative and attention grabbing, not a sales pitch of any kind, because people are tired of being sold.

You'll need more than one commercial.

Q. One of the biggest problems I have with my elevator speech is I'm never sure what to say. My company offers so many products and services that I haven't been able to come up with the perfect elevator speech.

I hate to break this to you, but there is no such thing as the perfect elevator speech. Your thirty-second commercial will never fit every situation. What you must do is design numerous elevator speeches for all the situations you might encounter. Here is an example of some of the different introductions you might need.

- Let's start with the easiest one. Make sure you always have a good commercial for each of the products or services you are promoting at the time. Your elevator speech needs to fit your current environment, or people won't understand what you are saying. For instance, if you know that you are going to be with a group of people that could use a particular service that you are offering, you'll want to use an elevator speech that best highlights that service and mentions the benefits that your service offers. If you attend another function where one of your products might be beneficial, you'll want to craft your elevator speech around that product and how it will benefit them.

- A more difficult elevator speech to create will be the one that tries to encompass all that you do. Many times, it is so difficult to make a commercial that addresses everything you do that you must take a more general approach and let people know more about who you are, not just what you do. With these types of commercials, you can really be imaginative and have fun.

The process of developing numerous elevator speeches is difficult and time consuming, but when you start meeting more people, making more connections, and selling more product, you'll see how powerful having the right elevator speech can be.

✔ **Action Plan:**

From this day forth, I will make sure I use a different elevator speech for each of the messages I'm trying to deliver because I don't want to dilute my own message by mentioning more than one thought at a time.

Off the cuff rarely works.

Q. When I do my elevator speech, I normally just make up something on the fly. What does this type of introduction do to my business?

An elevator speech is meant to help start the beginnings of a connection and possibly the beginnings of a great business relationship. However, most people never think about the possibility that their elevator speech could actually be HURTING their business.

I have seen so many people try to make up an elevator speech on the fly, and I can tell you that 99.9 percent of them STINK!! Why are these types of elevator speeches so bad? It's because they contain TMRT, which stands for "too many random thoughts." Allow me to explain.

When someone asks you what you do for a living, your mind is caught off guard and you're not sure what to say. Because of this, you start listing off all the things that you do and all the features or services that your company might offer. Unfortunately, these random thoughts seldom have a point or a direction, and you end up confusing your listener. By having a specific way to answer the question "what do you do," you will always be prepared to deliver the most effective and most captivating answer to this question.

Think about the actors in Hollywood. There are a few of them that can improvise their way through a scene. However, most actors that are working on a movie or a play have a script so they know exactly what they are going to say. Why is this? Because they must get the right point across to the audience so the entire story makes sense. You need to do the same thing for yourself and your business so people will start to learn your story, too.

✔ **Action Plan:**

From this day forth, I will always have an elevator speech ready to be delivered at a moment's notice. This way, I'll feel more comfortable meeting new people, and I might just pick up a bit of new business.

It's important to make them laugh.

Q. I think I'm a very funny person, but I seldom use my natural humor when I introduce myself to others. Is this a mistake?

I have always believed that there are people who are funny, and there are people who aren't. If you are one of those unfortunate few that doesn't have a funny bone in your body, please spare the rest of the human race, and don't try to be funny. A poor attempt at humor can actually hurt your potential connections with others, and it's painful for other people to listen to.

Now that I have properly upset all the non-funny people, let's talk about those of you that have a sense of humor. If you are one of those people that is naturally funny, your humor will do more for you and your business than you could ever believe. Why is this? Because when you make people laugh, smile, chuckle, or milk-through-the-nose hysterical, you make them feel more comfortable and more relaxed. One of the greatest gifts you can give to the people you meet is to make them feel comfortable around you. Once they are comfortable around you, they will become comfortable with you, and then they will listen to what you have to say.

Now that they are listening to you, how do you use your humor in your elevator speech? It's relatively simple if you know how to look at your job or your business in a funny way. Here are a few examples.

- Create a humorous title for your position such as The Queen of Clean™, The Mortgage Maven, King of the Hill (sells land), The Real Estate Guru, Head Bean Counter, or Professional Ice Breaker. (That one is mine.)

- Don't take yourself TOO seriously. Life is too darn short to be that serious about things. If you can learn to laugh at yourself, other people will get a kick out of your humor, too.

- Think about the things that are funny about your business or your industry. This has always been easy for lawyers, accountants, and Amway distributors, but more difficult for Realtors®, chiropractors, retail shop owners, and others. If you can find humor in your business, so will the people around you.

If you want to use more humor in your elevator speech, practice the funny stuff for one or two people before you unleash your hysteria on the masses. The one thing that will make people stop listening to what you have to say is BAD HUMOR.

✔**Action Plan:**

From this day forth, I will attempt to infuse as much humor as I can get away with into my elevator speech so I can better engage people's interest and help make people remember me. However, if I'm a truly unfunny person, I will not attempt to make people laugh, because that just doesn't work out well.

The KISS method always works.

Q. What's the best method to use so that my elevator speech is always clear and easy to understand?

A gentleman that I know has a great business. Every time he comes to a chamber function and it his time to deliver his thirty-second commercial, he stands up and goes into tremendous detail about the service that he offers and the benefits people will receive by working with him. He gets so deep into his topic that people no longer understand what the heck he is talking about.

I appreciate the fact that he tries to share so much information with us about what he does, but unfortunately, in thirty to sixty seconds, it is almost impossible for us to understand something at that depth. What you and my friend need to use is the famous KISS method, which means "Keep It Short and Simple."

The sooner you understand that most people need to hear your message as simply as possible, the sooner you'll start to engage more people in better conversations about YOUR business. If you talk about something that is difficult for them to understand, when people hear it for the first time, they will never come up to you and say, "Wait, backup, I didn't understand that. Could you please tell me that again?" Most people will say, "Huh, that's very interesting" and move on. They'll do this because they don't understand what you said to them, and people will never admit that they didn't understand what they just heard. If you always remember to keep your elevator speech short (thirty to forty-five seconds) and simple (so any ten-year-old kid could understand it), you'll find yourself creating a lot more connections.

✔ **Action Plan:**

From this day forth, I will make sure my thirty-second commercial will always be short and simple so that everyone who hears it will understand exactly what I do.

Sometimes less is more.

Q. When I have the opportunity to share my elevator speech with people, I tend to include lots of information so people will get the complete picture of what I really do. Is this the right way?

Let me start by saying that there isn't one right way to deliver an elevator speech. However, by practicing a few simple ideas, you'll find your introduction being more right than wrong.

Many people feel that if they only have thirty to sixty seconds to get their message across, they want to cram as much information as is humanly possible into those thirty to sixty seconds. You need to be very careful about the amount of information you provide in an elevator speech. As I have said before, most people will not be able to absorb or comprehend too much information. Trying to fill their heads with tremendous amounts of information is going to confuse people, and it is going to frustrate you, because you are not going to be earning the results that you want.

A good rule of thumb is to mention one very solid, easy-to-understand point and provide enough detail so that people will totally comprehend what you are saying. If you can get people to completely understand one part of your business and they become interested in what you do, they will ask you for more information. At this stage, they are ready, willing, and able to hear a lot more information.

One challenge that this rule of thumb creates is that, if you're talking to someone who isn't interested in your first

13

point, she might not take the time to learn about the other points that your business can offer. If this is the case, you must either develop many elevator speeches so you can use them where you think they might fit, or you can come up with one great commercial that will encompass the greatest general benefit that you provide to your listener. Regardless of the method you choose, if people walk away knowing one thing about your business, you are way ahead of the game.

✔ Action Plan:

From this day forth, I will provide just enough information in my elevator speech so people will have an idea of what I do. I will not provide too much information so that people believe they know enough to make a judgment about my business.

Dare to be different.

Q. The last time I attended a connection function, everyone stood up and gave the same type of commercial. If someone comes across as REALLY different, is that a good thing?

I have a simple answer for you. YES!!! Different is good. Different is attention grabbing. Different makes people sit up and take notice of the person who is breaking out of the mold.

One of the biggest problems with hearing an entire room full of elevator speeches, one after the other, is that you end up with a lot of "monkey see, monkey do" behavior. Most people are not prepared with what they are going to say, so they wing it. How do they wing it? They see how everyone else is doing their commercial, and they just follow suit. Unfortunately, this works against you because your elevator speech will be just like all the others.

I was at a chamber function about a month ago and a gentleman stood up to do his elevator speech. He stands in front of the audience and says absolutely nothing. After about twenty-five of his thirty seconds passed, he stated his name and company name and then said, "Dare to be different," and immediately sat down.

You can look at what this gentleman did from two different angles. You can say he wasted his thirty seconds by not saying anything about his business or his product or his service, but maybe all he wanted to do was get people to pay attention to him and remember him. Considering that this gentleman comes to this specific event regularly, people did pay attention to him and certainly remembered him. Here are a few ideas for making your elevator speech stand out from the crowd.

- Recite your elevator speech in a poem format, or turn your introduction into a short song, using a very familiar tune.

- Without saying a word, hold up clever signs that provide the audience with great information.

- When it's your turn to speak, recite your elevator speech from a different part of the room.

- Carefully chosen, a good prop will always grab the attention of the audience.

Different is good as long as it fits the environment. Step out of the norm, and people will always remember you.

✔ Action Plan:

From this day forth, I will always work to make my elevator speech as different and unique as possible so I can stand out from the crowd.

No pen means no notes.

Q. Do people ever write down any of the things I say when I do my elevator speech in front of a group?

FABULOUS QUESTION!! Thanks for asking it. When it comes to listening to your elevator speech, very few people will listen with a pen in hand. Traditionally, less than ten percent of the people in your audience will find what you are saying noteworthy. Because of this, be very careful about giving out too much information that listeners need to remember. This includes email addresses, locations of your business, phone numbers, websites, dates for upcoming programs, and anything else that includes very specific details.

If you want people to remember your vital information, make sure your elevator speech is captivating enough so that they must approach you after the program to ask for a card or ask for more details about your upcoming program or how they can start working with you.

✔ Action Plan:

From this day forth, I will only provide the kinds of information during my elevator speech that people don't have to be concerned about writing down.

9th Flr.

Make sure you edit your comments.

Q. Before I ask my question, allow me to confess that I am not a prude. With that said, what are your thoughts about people using off-color remarks or racy phrases to elicit a reaction from people?

When you have the opportunity to deliver your elevator speech to an individual or, even more important, before a large group, be very, very careful about using off-color or potentially offensive remarks to grab the audience's attention. I know a gentleman that typically includes some humor in his introduction, which is usually a good idea if it's done correctly. Unfortunately, his humor always ends up being of a quasi-sexual nature. He thinks it's hysterical, but this type of humor constantly makes his listeners uncomfortable.

In addition to off-color or inappropriate comments, be aware of comments that can potentially hurt people. A woman stood up at a chamber function that I attended and said that she worked for an Alzheimer's care facility. She paused then said, "I'm sorry but I have forgotten the rest." Many people thought it was funny, but considering that I lost a father-in-law to Alzheimer's, it wasn't funny to me or anyone else who has had to deal with this horrible disease.

One last example to help drive the point home is about a friend of mine who owns a food company that has a very delicious product. In describing the food, my friend often says this particular product is "better than sex." While most people would not be offended by this comment, if he does offend somebody, that person will never approach him and say, "By the way, you offended me with your comment the other day." The person simply won't ever buy his product or service and may possibly recommend that other people do the same.

Always remember that using humor and catchy phrases in your elevator speech is a great way to grab people's attention, but be careful, because your humor could be turning people off, and you will never even know it.

✔ **Action Plan:**

From this day forth, I will always be aware of the people around me and do what I can not to offend or upset them with my elevator speech.

10th Flr.

Your elevator speech can kill or create a relationship.

Q. I've had the opportunity to hear some REALLY bad elevator speeches. Some have been so bad that I will NEVER do business with these people. How do I avoid having my elevator speech drive people away from my business and me?

I do not ever want you to underestimate the power of a good elevator speech. The way you answer the question, "What do you do?" could potentially begin a very profitable and enjoyable business and/or personal relationship in your life. However, if people ask you what you do, and you give them an answer that they do not like, for whatever reason, it could end up killing the beginning of that relationship.

What are some of the ways that your elevator speech can drive people away from you? Here are a few examples.

- If people ask you what you do and you immediately launch into a hard-core sales pitch, you have just put them on the defensive. Think about how you feel when someone starts acting very pushy and only wants to sell you her product or service. Is this someone with whom you want to be doing business? I don't think so. What makes it even worse for the pushy sales person is that you will tell everyone you know to avoid her because you don't want your friends to be pressured either.

- Be careful not to have an elevator speech that is so canned or phony or so unbelievable that people immediately have doubts about you and your business. When I talk to people and they make their product or service seem bigger than life, I start to wonder if they can really do what they claim they can do. As I've said before, you want to provide people with enough information so that they can learn about your business but not so much that they can make an incorrect judgment.

- How does it feel when someone comes up to you and shoves one of his business cards into your hand? Most people will take the card because they want to be polite, but they did not want the card in the first place. Most of these cards will end up in the trashcan. I suggest that you NEVER start your elevator speech with a business card. If your introduction is good, people will ask you for your card. Also, if you wait for people to ask for your card, you'll save a fortune on printing costs.

If you start being careful about how you answer the question, "What do you do?" you will find yourself meeting and connecting with more people than ever before, and you will avoid the possibility of forever tainting a potentially prosperous relationship.

✔**Action Plan:**

From this day forth, I will make sure that my elevator speech is doing everything possible to draw more people toward me so I can make great connections with them and grow my business much faster.

No reaction means an ineffective elevator speech.

Q. I think I'm doing something wrong. Often when I say my elevator speech, I get little to no reaction from people. How can I change that?

If you've ever given your thirty-second commercial to people, and, when you were finished, they stared at you like stunned sheep or a deer caught in headlights, you've wasted an opportunity to make a new connection with those people.

Many people develop elevator speeches that are confusing, complicated, and unclear. The best way to see if your message is getting across to people is to see how they react after you say your introduction. Here are a few examples of the reactions you might see.

- If the people you are talking to look like bobble heads with their heads bobbing up and down, almost uncontrollably, I can guarantee you that they are thinking, "What the heck did you just say? I don't understand it." They don't want to appear ignorant, so they pretend that they know what you are talking about, even though they don't.

- You can almost always tell if people are no longer listening to you by watching their eyes. If people begin your conversation looking you in the eyes and then they start looking around and not paying as much attention to you, this is your signal to stop talking and get these people back on the same page as you.

The problem you face when you lose people during your elevator speech is that they will never say, "Wait a minute...I didn't catch that....could you please say that again?" They will smile at you and look for any opportunity to break away and talk to other people that won't confuse them.

■ One of the best ways to see if your commercial is hitting home is if people nod their heads as you speak, give you an "mmm hmm," or any other acknowledgement noise that indicates they are interested, show you a little smile or a laugh, or provide any other signal that they are still with you.

The more of a reaction you get from people, the better your elevator speech was. The less reaction you get, the worse your elevator speech was. People's reactions are your barometer as to how well your message came across to them.

✔ **Action Plan:**
From this day forth, I will be much more aware of how people are reacting while I'm delivering my elevator speech, because the better the reactions, the better results I'll receive.

Job hunters need a great introduction, too.

Q. I am currently between careers. While all the info you provide is very helpful, how can it help me since I don't have a job?

One of the greatest misconceptions for job hunters in the world today is that they don't have to have an effective elevator speech unless they are currently working. This notion couldn't be further from the truth. If you are looking for a job, it's imperative that you have a simple and direct message for people when they ask you what you do. Here are a few ideas for you.

- The first thing you have to tell people is that you are looking for work. Some of you are probably saying, "DUH!" but I can't tell you how many job seekers are too embarrassed to inform people they're looking for work. One of the biggest challenges is how to say you're unemployed. Try saying, "I'm currently between employment opportunities," or, "I'm currently searching for that next great employment adventure," or simply state the fact that you are seeking the right position. Being unemployed isn't viewed the same way it was twenty years ago. With the massive layoffs and the corporate downsizing, people are far more empathetic towards your situation. Always remember that if people don't know you're looking for something, THEY CAN'T HELP YOU FIND IT!!

■ Speaking of helping, the best thing you can do with your elevator speech is to provide enough information so that it's easy for people to help you. How do you do this? Provide them with as much detail as possible about your job search. If people ask you what kind of job you are looking for, don't say "something in high tech" or "something in management." These responses are far too vague for most people. If you want a job in high tech, name specific companies you would like to work for or specific projects or products with which you would like to be involved. Most people are more than willing to help you, but you must at least meet them halfway. Don't make them do all the work.

■ My last recommendation is that you take your newly developed elevator speech, attend as many connection functions as possible, and use your perfectly crafted speech!! Thousands of people are mass mailing their resumes to companies, but less than seven percent of jobs are found this way. Thousands more are looking for work through the newspaper, but less than nine percent of jobs are found this way. Millions of people are spending days on the computer looking for that perfect job on the Internet, but only fifteen percent of jobs are ever found using this method. The very best way to find that perfect job is to meet people and let them know who you are and why they should hire you.

✔ Action Plan:

From this day forth, I will use an elevator speech to provide people I meet with enough information about my job hunt so they can help me without having to work too hard.

Section Two

13th Flr.

Your typical opening just isn't cutting it.

Q. I firmly believe you only get one chance to make a great first impression. When I meet people and introduce myself, is it important to tell them my name, my title, and the company I work for?

I hate to be the one to break this to you, but when it comes to delivering your elevator speech, no one really cares who you are, what you do, or where you work! I don't mean to sound harsh or disrespectful. What I want you to understand is that until you give people a reason to listen to you, they won't! You might be asking, what's wrong with this type of introduction? Allow me to explain why this type of opening for your elevator speech is ineffective.

- An acronym I use when I'm evaluating elevator speeches is "3M," and it has nothing to do with Minnesota Mining and Manufacturing, the company that was founded in 1902 at the Lake Superior town of Two Harbors, Minnesota. "3M," to me, stands for "ME, ME, ME." Starting your elevator speech by reciting your name, title, and company name puts all the attention on you and not your listener. To grab people's attention and keep a solid hold on it, you need to use words like "you" and "yours."

- When people introduce themselves to me, it takes me a few seconds to focus in on what they are saying. Unfortunately, by the time I'm ready to listen, they have said their name, title, and company name, and I've missed all of it. Remembering people's names is a very hard job. By telling people who you are right up front, you are actually making it harder for them to remember you.

- If you are delivering your elevator speech in front of a group of people and you start with your name, title, and company name, by the time you reach the end of your introduction, the audience has completely forgotten who you are. This is especially problematic if you have said something fascinating and audience members want to talk to you. Since most people are very nervous about meeting people they don't know, they typically won't approach you to learn more about you.

If you are one of those people that has to start your elevator speech with your name, title, and company name, that's okay, but please understand that you are doing a disservice to yourself and your business. People want eventually to know your information but knowing when to provide it is half the battle.

✔ Action Plan:

From this day forth, I will not start my elevator speech with my name, title, and company name, because people are concerned with what I can do for them before they care about what they can do for me.

Only use words that everyone will understand.

Q. I work in an industry that is very complicated and confusing. Our biggest challenge is trying to get people to understand what we do. Any suggestions?

Did you know that the average newspaper is written at a fifth-grade reading level? The *New York Times*, that highbrow newspaper, is written at an eighth-grade reading level. As you can see, people have become accustomed to reading the written word and hearing spoken language at levels that everybody can understand.

If you happen to be one of those people that likes to speak using long, complicated words and a somewhat confusing vocabulary—what I refer to as twenty-five-cent words— you are risking the possibility of people not understanding what you are saying. In your mind, you are using vocabulary that is simple and easy to understand. It's only simple to you because you use words like this every single day. If you come from a highly technical industry or one of those businesses in which people have a hard time grasping what you really do, you need to use the simplest words possible when you deliver your elevator speech.

As I have mentioned before, if you use words or phrases that people don't understand, they will seldom ask you to explain what you just said. People don't like to admit that they didn't understand something. They typically just nod their heads and wonder what the heck you are talking about. If you have a choice between a word that might make you sound very intelligent but might potentially confuse your listeners and a less complex word, always choose the word that is easier to understand. I am not encouraging you to dumb down your elevator speech. All I'm saying is that the simpler you make it, the better people will understand it, and the more they understand it, the more likely they are to be doing business with you.

✔ Action Plan:

From this day forth, I will always use the simplest form of a word so people will easily understand what I'm talking about.

Leave the industry buzzwords within your industry.

Q. I have given my elevator speech many times, but I always get the feeling that people don't really understand what I do? What am I doing wrong?

You aren't doing anything wrong. What you are probably doing is using TMBW, which stands for Too Many Buzz Words. Many times when people give their elevator speech, they use words that are very recognizable in their industry but that are completely unknown to the rest of the world. Here are a few examples.

- **Baby Bells**—A common nickname given to the United States regional telephone companies that were formed from the breakup of AT&T in 1984, which was done to create more competition within the industry.

- **Forensic Accounting**—Forensic Accounting utilizes accounting, auditing, and investigative skills to conduct an examination into a company's financial statements, thus providing an accounting analysis that is suitable for court.

- **Killer Applications**—Killer application or "killer app" is a buzzword that describes a software application that surpasses all of its competitors.

- **The New Paradigm**—In the investing world, a totally new way of doing things that has a huge effect on business.

- **Ponzi Scheme**—A fraudulent investing scam that promises high rates of return at little risk to investors. The scheme generates return by way of acquiring new investors.

- **Risk Capital**—The money that a person allocates to investing in high-risk securities.

To be honest with you, the term "elevator speech" is an industry buzzword. When I say that I wrote a book on elevator speeches, many people look at me and say, "What the heck is an elevator speech?" This is why I also call them thirty-second commercials or business introductions, as well as a few other terms.

The goal of your elevator speech is to use terms and phrases that almost anyone will understand. How can you expect people to ask for more information about your business if they really have NO idea of what you do?

For people that have real trouble trying not to use typical industry buzzwords, there is a great website called www.Investopedia.com, which lists hundreds of industry buzzwords and supplies a much simpler explanation of the words. Check it out, and you'll find more people understanding what you do.

✔ Action Plan:

From this day forth, I will stop using the buzzwords from my specific industry when I'm telling people my elevator speech, because I don't want to confuse people or make them feel uneducated.

Do everything you can to make your name memorable.

Q. My last name is Smith. There are millions of Smiths out there. What can I do to help people remember my name better?

I know a gentleman by the name of Jim Rosenfield. Jim is an insurance agent. As you know, there are a million insurance agents. So what does Jim do to help people remember his name? As I said, his last name is Rosenfield. Every time Jim says his elevator speech, he says, "My name is Jim Rosenfield. I am the Rose in the field of insurance, that is, a Rose in the field of insurance—Rosenfield." He gives people an easy way to remember his name.

Unfortunately, this doesn't work with every name. Let's take my last name, which is Sherman. Should I say something like, "I'm the MAN that likes to say SURE a lot?" Just doesn't have the same impact, does it?

Try to come up with a way to help people remember your name. An elevator speech is only as good as it is memorable. If you can create something that is clever, unique, or even tells a story, and make that part of your elevator speech, people are going to come and talk to you, because they will remember who you are.

Allow me to share one last comment about names. I am often asked about how to remember people's names. I'm not very good at this, but I'm getting better. Here are two techniques I like to use.

1. Face association. Examine a person's face discretely when you are introduced. Try to find an unusual feature, whether ears, hairline, forehead, eyebrows, eyes, nose, mouth, chin, or complexion.

   Create an association between that characteristic of the face and the name in your mind. Possibly associate the person with someone you know with the same name, or maybe associate a rhyme or image from the name with the person's face or defining feature.

2. Repetition. When you are introduced, ask for the name to be repeated. Use the name yourself as often as possible (without overdoing it!). If it is unusual, ask how it is spelled or where it is comes from, and if appropriate, exchange cards. The more often you hear and see the name, the more likely it is to sink in.

Also, after you have left that person's company, review the name in your mind several times. If you are particularly keen, you might decide to make notes. (Thank you Mind Tools Ltd. for this valuable information.)

✔ Action Plan:

From this day forth, I will try to make myself more memorable by using any technique possible that will help people remember my name.

A good prop always works.

Q. When I'm delivering my elevator speech to a group, is there a surefire way to grab the audience's attention quickly?

When you are telling people about your product or service, it is always a great idea to let them see your product or service. However, if you happen to be in a business that sells a product or service that can't be seen (insurance, financial planning, consulting, etc.), you need to discover some sort of prop that will help people better grasp what you really do.

What kind of props am I talking about? Here are a few examples.

- A woman I know sells health insurance. When she does her elevator speech, she holds up a toy ambulance and presses a button so the siren sounds. She then says, "You never want to hear this noise. But, if you do, you want to make sure you're properly covered." It is a great example, and it drives the point home.

- A chiropractor once stood up in front of the room with a skeleton's spine. He twisted it and bent it over and really abused it. He then said, "If your back ever feels like this, you need to be talking to me."

- A man I know that owns a sign shop walked up to the front of the room and held up a very ugly sign for a restaurant and said, "This was a client's sign before using Sign-o-Rama." He then held up another beautiful, colorful, and effective sign and said, "This is my client's sign after using Sign-o-Rama."

If you happen to be lucky enough to have a product that you can show to people, always make sure you carry your product with you and use it during your elevator speech. I know a woman who sells a very clever pop-up advertising display. She just opens the bag, and the sign springs to life. It's quite an attention grabber, and people see exactly what she is selling.

The easier and clearer you make your message, the better chance you have of making a good connection with people. Once they understand what you really do, they can start telling their connections about you.

✔ **Action Plan:**

From this day forth, I will be on the lookout for any type of prop that will help me grab the attention of the people I'm talking to and help to educate them about what I do.

Pictures speak more than a thousand words.

Q. I own a painting business, and it's very hard to explain to people why I'm different from the hundreds of other painters out there. Any suggestions as to how I can stand out from the crowd?

To answer your question, I have three words for you and for anyone else in a beautification business: Before and After. I am assuming that the things you work on look better when they are done than before you started. (If they don't, I suggest you enroll in truck driving school... HA HA HA.) All you need to do is take a picture of what you are working on before you start and take another picture after you are done. Then, when people ask you what you do, just whip out your little album and show them. Allow me to share a few examples to help illustrate my point.

- Living in Arizona, our backyards are surrounded by fence walls. I know a gentleman that paints beautiful murals on these walls that make the backyard look so much better. When you see the "after" pictures, you immediately know what he does.

- I know an auto detailer that can make any car look like a million bucks. He makes my car look so good, I'm never going to sell it. He takes a before picture of every car he works on so he can show people the magic he can create when he is done.

- Here is another Arizona example. Due to the hot summer, you must have a pool in your backyard or you will DIE, or at least get really, really sweaty. To show people what they can do with almost any sized backyard, the pool company that did our pool always carries a photo album so people can see how beautiful their pools can be.

If you are in a business where a picture will tell what you do much better than you can verbally describe it, always make sure you have that album of pictures close by to show anyone that asks you, "What do you do?"

✔ Action Plan:

From this day forth, I will start using pictures to help drive home my message about what I do when I share my elevator speech with others.

The price is not always right.

Q. What are your thoughts about whether people should mention pricing in their elevator speeches?

This has always been the $64,000 question. Should I or shouldn't I talk about price? My answer to this question is how I feel about this issue. Many people might feel differently, but after hearing thousands and thousands of thirty-second commercials, I feel that you should not mention pricing.

When people talk about pricing in their elevator speech, they are "showing their hand too early," as they say in the poker world. When you mention price to people before they know about your product or service, they are going to make a judgment immediately as to whether your product or service is worth the price that you are putting on it. Unfortunately, they are making these judgments based on absolutely no realistic information. Here are a few examples.

- We'll detail your car inside and out for $199

- You can get a beautiful website starting at only $799

- Send a delicious box of fudge for only $39.95

Once people hear the prices, they'll immediately say to themselves, "Do I think that product or service is worth that price?" If they don't know much about your company, most likely, they will think the price is too high.

The only time a price should be used is if you are running a very specific, very attractive special. For instance, I have written two books, in addition to this one. They are titled *50 TOP TIPS, A Simple Guide to Networking Success* and

Breaking the Ice, 306 Great Conversation Starters. Traditionally, the cost for both of these books is $32, but I am selling both of them for only $20. This is a great deal. (If you want to take advantage of this great deal, please go to www.ConnectionPros.com, and click on the online store link.) Because it's such a great deal, I sometimes use that as my elevator speech. It works because the message of the great deal stands on its own two feet.

✔ Action Plan:

From this day forth, I will give serious thought before mentioning anything about price or cost when I say my elevator speech so people don't make a value judgment about my business before they know the whole story.

Be careful of the 3Ms.

Q. When I'm writing my elevator speech, are there any words that I should shy away from using?

When I listen to endless elevator speeches and make notes about the things that people should change to make their commercial more effective, I often use the abbreviation 3M, which stands for "Me, Me, Me." Anytime you start an elevator speech with "I" or "we," and you continually use "I" and "we" and "me" throughout the elevator speech, people are going to stop listening to you because, to be blunt, they do not care about you. They only care about themselves.

You must make sure that when you deliver your elevator speech, instead of using the words "I," "me," and "we," you use the words "you," "yours," and other words that refer to the listener. Here are a few examples:

Instead of saying

- We design computer software for small companies.

- I train people how to speak better in public.

- My company sells and services copy and fax machines.

Try saying

- Your small business needs the best computer software, and we can help design it for you.

- Your business will really fly if you learn how to speak better in public and I can help you.

- You need the best fax and copy machines to keep your company moving. We can help you with that.

As you can see, I'm still using the words I, me, or we, but they are only mentioned after I mention you or yours. When you are talking to others about your product or service, the more times you can say "you," and focus your message on the benefits people will receive, the more these people will listen to you, and the more engaging your commercial will be.

✔**Action Plan:**

From this day forth, I will use the words "you" and "yours" more often that I use the words "I" or "me" or "we" so people will be more engaged by my elevator speech because it is about them, not me.

Everyone offers good service.

Q. Every time I hear an elevator speech, about half of the people say something about providing good service. Since everyone says it, does it lose its impact?

I have a challenge for you. I dare you to grab any *Yellow Pages* and open up to any of the display ads; I will bet you $100—all right, maybe not $100—but I bet that one of the ads on the pages will mention something about providing "good service," "superior service," "quality service," or some other usage of the word "service."

You will notice that companies say they have good service because they think that promise will draw people in. What do they think—that if the words are not written there, people are going to think that they have bad service? Very doubtful!!

Good service is something that has been overused for far too long. When you present an elevator speech, do not use the words, "We offer good service," "quality service," or "excellent service," because until I use your product or service, I do not know how good your services can really be. What you need to do is convince me that what you offer is so engaging and so worthwhile to me that I am willing to listen to more. Your claim of quality service is not going to close the deal with me.

Furthermore, I believe most businesses offer good service until they show me that they don't. I've been called a Pollyanna in my life, but I believe that most businesses provide the kind of service that will keep bringing me back. If many other people are like me (oh, God forbid), they, too, will believe you will provide them with great service.

Always remember that quality service is not going to make me call you and say, "Hi, I want to do business with you." The benefits of what you offer and how it can help me are what are going to draw me through the door.

✔ Action Plan:

From this day forth, I will not mention anything about the level of service I provide when I deliver my elevator speech, because people need to experience good service, not hear about it.

Always remember your name.

Q. What is one of the biggest mistakes people make when they are delivering their elevator speech?

A few months ago, I was attending a networking function, and all the attendees had the chance to stand up and deliver their elevator speech. Unfortunately, most of them were terrible, but there was one guy who was fabulous. Everything he said was perfect. He focused on the benefits, kept it short and simple, and ended with a great tag line. The only thing he missed was his own name. That caused a major problem, because I wanted to see him after the program, and since he left early, I never had the chance to congratulate him on having the best introduction in the group. I also wanted to learn more about his business but didn't know his name so that I could follow up with him.

I cannot begin to tell you how many elevator speeches I have heard where people have told me great things about their companies, the wonderful things that they could offer me, and why their business would benefit me, yet the thing that they forgot to tell me at the end was their name. Many times, I will walk up to someone whose elevator speech I have heard and ask him for his name. However, most people are too uncomfortable approaching people they do not know. If you want people to walk up to you and talk to you about your product or service, you must make sure you give them your name. Omitting it is a simple mistake to make, especially if you are nervous, but a mistake like this can cost you more than you'll ever know.

✔ **Action Plan:**

From this day forth, I will always remember to say my name when I'm presenting my thirty-second commercial to a group of people so they will know who I am and will feel more comfortable when they approach me.

It is not the length that counts.

Q. My business has been around for more than thirty years. Is this a piece of information that I should include in my elevator speech?

You've heard it a thousand times: people mentioning how many years they've been in business.

- "I have been in business twenty-five years."

- "My company's been helping people for thirty-five years."

- "We've been serving the valley for fifty years."

When you are delivering your elevator speech and you are informing people about your company for the first time, very few people will hire you because you have been in business a long time. I am not minimizing the importance of a company that has been in business a long time. Longevity is very valuable, something that will benefit you tremendously. However, it will only benefit you once people start to explore your company more deeply, and the way that exploration can begin is with a killer elevator speech.

By telling people the number of years you have been in business, you believe that people are saying to themselves, "Wow, they've been in business a long time. Let's go buy from them." But in *their* minds they are thinking, "Why are you telling me this? I really don't care." If you have been in business for thirty-five years, that is great. But what can those thirty-five years of experience do to benefit your listener?

The length of time you have been in business is a terrific way to reinforce people's decision to do business with you. Once people know the benefits you offer, the products and services you have available, and the great staff that you have working for you, your business tenure will support the strength of your business and encourage people to buy from you.

✔ Action Plan:

From this day forth, I will wait to make the beginnings of a connection with someone before I start talking about how long I've been in business. In this way, my longevity in business will help build a deeper and more fruitful relationship.

Mention your businesses one at a time.

Q. Besides my full time job, I have a small consulting business on the side. How can I let people know about both of my businesses in my elevator speech?

In today's economic environment, most people are working harder and longer than ever. Some people have a full-time job and a part-time business. Some people have two full-time businesses. I once read a statistic that blew my mind. Do you realize that almost seventy percent of the people in the United States have a second job or a part-time business on the side? No wonder people are so rushed and frantic all the time.

While it's very important to you to let people know about everything you do, there is only so much information they can absorb. The biggest mistake you can make is trying to mention your multiple jobs or businesses in one elevator speech. When you do this, in your mind, you think that you come across as worldly and having a lot to offer, that people are going to say, "Well, isn't that interesting! Please tell me about both of your businesses." What actually happens is you end up confusing people because they don't know what you really do.

Here is what typically happens. You'll say something like the following:

I work for a small telecommunications company that helps people save money on their phone bills each month. I also own a graphic design business that does business cards, letterhead, and custom logos.

Do you see the words "I also..." in the above example? What those two words really say is, "Please forget everything I just said, and only remember what I'm about to tell you now." When you tell them about your first business and then immediately start telling them about your second business, they will forget most of what you said in the beginning and only remember the information at the end, because they have not had the time to transfer that first part into their long-term memory. Please understand that most people don't listen that closely to what you are saying anyway. So why compound that problem by giving them too much information?

To overcome this problem, develop separate elevator speeches for each of your businesses. This way, each one of your professions can get the attention that it deserves. If that is too difficult for you, try to develop a commercial that can encompass the benefits that both of your professions offer without diluting your message with too much specific information about both businesses.

✔ Action Plan:

From this day forth, I will only mention one business per elevator speech so I don't dilute my message or confuse my listeners.

Beware of the SRQ.

Q. I see many people starting off their elevator speech with some sort of question. Is this a good way to get started?

Many times people will start an elevator speech by rattling off a bunch of questions such as

- "How many of you would like to earn more money?"

- "Who would like to have more time in their life?"

- "How many of you have too much stress in your life?"

These are questions that everybody would obviously answer in the same way, which is why I refer to them as SRQ— "Stupid Rhetorical Questions." Okay, that might have been a bit too harsh, so let's call them "Standard Rhetorical Questions." A rhetorical question is the type that you really don't want people to answer. They are used to get people to start thinking about the message behind the question, not the question itself.

You'll want to avoid questions like these at all times because, most likely, people have heard them so many times, they will immediately stop listening. The more times you use SRQs, the less people are listening. The questions also chew up valuable time when you are trying to deliver your elevator speech.

If you want to use a rhetorical question, use a question that truly has relevant meaning to your message and is not the same type of question that you've heard a million times before. Always remember to give some sort of answer to your rhetorical question at the end of your elevator speech.

One last comment for you: If you want to use SRQs, please only use one per commercial. As I've said before, people can only remember so much, and they will never remember more than one SRQ at a time.

✔ Action Plan:

From this day forth, if I need to use an SRQ in my elevator speech, I will make sure it's relevant to my message, and I will only include one.

Let your business card provide the details.

Q. When I tell people my elevator speech, I often include my website, phone number, and sometimes even my business location. Is there anything wrong with this?

One of the biggest mistakes people make when they give their thirty-second commercials at a chamber event or at a leads group is to include the address or location of their business. When was the last time you watched people whip out a pen to immediately write down notes about your elevator speech? It's hard enough to get people to listen to what you saying. Expecting them to take notes is a real pipe dream. You typically have only thirty to sixty seconds to get your message across to people. Since you don't want to waste any precious time, I suggest you let your business card provide the 411 about you.

I'm assuming that you have one of those little rectangular paper things (business cards) in your pocket that you like to give to people so they know who you are. If you take a look at this little rectangular thing, you'll notice it contains all the information people would want to know about you so they can contact you to learn more about your business. So, let your card do the talking about your location, and use those few extra seconds to mention another benefit of your business.

✔ **Action Plan:**

From this day forth, I will not mention my phone number, website, e-mail address, or business location when I'm delivering my elevator speech. I will let my business card provide all the details.

People really only care about the benefits you offer.

Q. I've always learned that I need to talk about features and benefits when I tell people about my business. Does this rule apply when I do my elevator speech?

When you ask most people what they do for a living, they have a tendency to ramble on and on about all the things their company does. Unfortunately, what they are normally rambling about is all the features that their company provides. The challenge you face is that no one really cares about the features of your business yet. They typically don't know anything about you and don't want to know that much about your business.

What people say when talking about their business is

- Our company does four color brochures
- We provide financial services for small businesses
- I buy and sell homes

Please don't think that I'm picking on these few occupations. EVERYONE from almost any industry does this.

If you really want to grab peoples' attention and make them listen to your elevator speech, you must completely focus on what benefit you are bringing to them. All people want to know is WIIFM, which means "WHAT'S IN IT FOR ME?" If you spend more time talking about how your business will help them and make their lives easier, people will stop and listen.

Using the above examples, here is what I would say that would focus on the benefits instead of the features.

- Our company specializes in creating four-color brochures *so your company will always look great in print.*

- We provide financial services for small businesses like yours *so that someday you'll be a big business.*

- I buy and sell homes *so you can get the home of your dreams and not have to do all the work.*

As you can see, the main focus is on the listener, not on your company. Spend more time working on the needs of your listeners, and they will take more time to listen to you.

✔ **Action Plan:**

From this day forth, I will only focus on what benefits I can bring to people instead of all the features that my company can offer.

Being different makes you more memorable.

Q. Every time I hear people deliver an elevator speech, they always seem to start with their name, their title, and their company name. Is this the way I should start my elevator speech?

You asked a great question. I've heard more elevator speeches in the past five years than most people will hear in a lifetime. Out of all of those pitches, more than ninety percent of them have started with name, title, and company name. Here are a few examples.

- Hi, my name is John Williamson. I'm a CPA for Williamson and Associates.

- I'm Joanne, and I work for Ballentine Motors.

- My name is Pete, and I'm an account executive for the XYZ Group.

Are these people wrong for starting their elevator speech that way? NO!! However, if everyone starts his commercial the same way, people will stop listening after a while, and that's the worst thing that can happen to you.

Another challenge that you face is that by giving your name and your company name in the beginning, most people will forget your name by the end of your commercial. If your elevator speech is truly engaging and people become interested in your product or service, many of them will think, "Wow, I should talk to her. By the way, what was her name?"

So, if you shouldn't start with your name and company name, what should you start with? Try to come up with something clever to really grab people's attention. You can ask a rhetorical question. You can start with a quote or a statistic. Whatever you start with, always remember that if you don't grab people's attention right away, you've lost them.

✔ Action Plan:

From this day forth, I will create an elevator speech that is different from the hundreds of other elevator speeches that I have heard.

Don't bury the best parts.

Q. I'm always confused about where I should put the best parts of my elevator speech. The beginning is always good, or should I save it until the end?

When I'm hired to do elevator speech evaluations for an organization, I use the acronym BBP, which stands for Buried Best Part. I use this acronym if I hear people saving the best piece of their commercial until the very end. A few chapters ago, I mentioned that you need to have a great opening. If there is something that you offer, or if your product or service is really unique, you should always start with this, because people will be intrigued by what you have said, and they will listen attentively to the rest of your elevator speech. However, if you start your introduction with your name, title, and company, most people will be so bored that they will have stopped listening by the time you get to the best part of your message.

How do you identify the best part of your message? Listen for the words that create some sort of reaction from the listener. If you say something and people laugh or smile or have some other reaction that says, "I heard what you said," that's an important part of your elevator speech. The more reaction you get while reciting your commercial, the better the outcome will be.

Another way to find out the best part of your message is to ask people. If you are talking to people you know, ask them what part of your elevator speech made their ears perk up. Most of the time, it will be a totally different part than you thought it would be. When I sold advertising in the early nineties, I learned to never fall in love with my own words. While I think what I'm saying is brilliant and fabulous, the only thing that matters is if your listener thinks what you are saying is brilliant and fabulous.

✔ Action Plan:

From this day forth, I will listen very closely to the reactions of the people hearing my elevator speech so I can better identify the best parts of my introduction.

30th Flr.

Always try to create mental pictures.

Q. What is one of the very best ways to get people to really understand what you do for a living?

One of the greatest ways to get your message across to people is to give them a mental picture of what you do in their heads. When you deliver an elevator speech that creates an image in your listeners' minds about how your product or service will best benefit them, they will understand what you do. More importantly, they will remember what you do. In addition, they will remember your information longer. Here are a few examples of how you can create mental pictures.

If you are a financial planner and you work with a lot of people that are saving money for retirement, you don't stand up and say, "Hi, my name is Bob, and I help people with their retirement." You need to create a mental picture of how people might spend their retirement, such as, "Imagine golfing every day and living in that perfect house right on the water. If you make sure your money is invested properly, you can retire and have this kind of life."

People in the travel business who say things like, "Hi, I'm a travel agent, and we can help you book your cruises and tickets and things such as that," are wasting their time. They need to be creating word pictures about the exotic places people want to go. They might say something like, "I want you to close your eyes and imagine yourself lying on the beaches of Hawaii, soaking up the sun, and sipping on a Piña Colada. How about snorkeling at the Great Barrier Reef in Australia and seeing every type of colorful fish

swim right in front of your face? Or picture yourself standing on the famous seventh tee box at Pebble Beach and
watching your golf ball land softly on the green and roll
into the hole."

These are the types of mental pictures people dream up
everyday. If you can get people to think about you when
they see these mental pictures, you are well on your way to
a very successful elevator speech.

✔ Action Plan:

From this day forth, I will try to incorporate mental
pictures into my elevator speech so people can visual-
ize what I can do for them before I have to tell them.

Who a good client is for you is meaningless for us.

Q. I belong to a leads group and I often hear people say, "A good client for me is..." when they are doing their elevator speech. What are your thoughts about this?

Before I answer your question, allow me to explain what a leads group is for those of you that have never heard this term before.

A leads group is a group of business people that meets at the same time and place on a weekly, biweekly, or monthly basis to encourage the exchange of business leads between the members. It is very important to get to know as much as possible about the other members' businesses and for other members to know as much as possible about yours. Members put substantial pressure on each other to generate leads for one another. Some groups even charge a small fine if you don't bring in leads.

These groups normally comprise one business professional from each chosen field, eliminating the competition for specific business leads. Other groups place restrictions on the length of time you are in business, or the level of responsibility you hold in a firm, when deciding who to accept for membership. Restrictions are placed on group membership to ensure it is composed of business professionals who are looking for the same thing and playing by the same rules.

One of the challenges faced by people who attend connection functions, as well as leads groups, is that they have a tendency to say, "a good client for me is...." when they are giving their elevator speech. I always encourage people not to use this phrase because, unless I know who you are and the type of work you do and why I should be referring business to you, I don't care what makes a good client for you. I have a very strict rule about the people to whom I refer business. I need to know them very well and know they are the best in their field, because the job they do has a major impact on my relationship with the people I send to them. If someone does a terrible job for the people I send to him or her, it makes me look bad, and I can't have that.

Another thing to remember is that if you are always telling people what a good client is for you, before they get to know you, you will start to develop a reputation as someone who only wants to sell his or her product or service to people and not someone who might be a good person with whom people can create a relationship.

✔ Action Plan:

From this day forth, I will always remember not to tell people what a good client for me might be since they have NO idea who I am and shouldn't be referring business to me until they do.

Watch the number of acronyms you use.

Q. I hope I'm not the only person that goes through this, but I get so confused with all the initials people use when they are talking about their business.

When I'm doing a presentation and someone mentions a specific acronym, I immediately stop the person and ask the audience how many people know what that acronym means. Typically, at least one-third of the audience is unaware of the meaning of that acronym. In other words, one-third of the people are now confused.

Many people work in industries where initials are used to describe something with which everyone in that industry is familiar. This happens very often for people in the high tech industry. It seems like every third word in high tech is based on some set of initials. Here are a few examples of acronyms that I hear everyday.

- IT—Information Technology
- HR—Human Resources
- RFP—Request for Proposal
- ROI—Return on Investment
- And SO many more

A good rule of thumb would be to never use an industry acronym unless you are speaking only to people from your industry. If there are people from other industries, state the whole phrase, so that everyone will understand you. Unfortunately, very few people will ever approach you to ask you to explain the acronym you used, because they don't want to potentially embarrass themselves.

Besides industry acronyms, be careful of association acronyms, too. If you are involved with any type of association, you probably refer to your association using an acronym. Here are a few examples.

- NSA—National Speakers Association
- MPI—Meeting Planners International
- ASTD—American Society of Training and Development
- ACCE—Association of Chamber of Commerce Executives
- NACE—National Association of Catering Executives
- And thousands of others

You need to make sure that you don't use these acronyms unless you are 110 percent certain that everybody in that audience knows what you are talking about. If you don't, they will become confused and uninterested and will stop listening to you.

✔Action Plan:

From this day forth, I will always remember not to use acronyms in my elevator speech, which could decrease the understanding of the audience.

The most powerful word in elevator speeches.

Q. I often hear people offer something for free when they share their introduction with people. Does this technique really work?

People are exposed to thousands and thousands of advertising messages each week. There is one word that is used in advertising that is more powerful than any other. It is the one word that will grab people's attention and have them listening to every word that comes out of your mouth. What is that word? That word is FREE.

When people hear this word, the first thing most people think is that they can get something for nothing. Researching the definition of the word free, I was surprised to discover that the definition "not costing or charging anything" was listed tenth out of fifteen definitions. Most of the definitions were based on the idea of FREEDOM. Here are a few examples.

- Having the legal and political rights of a citizen
- Not determined by anything beyond its own nature or being
- Relieved from or lacking something unpleasant or burdensome
- Having a scope not restricted by qualification

Why am I sharing this information with you? Does it have anything to do with your elevator speech? ABSOLUTELY NOT! I just thought it was interesting, and since this is my book, I can put in anything I want to. NEENER, NEENER, NEENER! Sorry about that last comment. My mind took a small detour. Let's get back to the subject at hand.

If you have a product or a service where you can offer a free sample, or a free appointment, or a free evaluation of your product or service, make sure everyone you talk to knows this. People always want to try something before they buy it, and if you are the person that offers this free sample, you'll do much more business. Here are examples to help spark a few ideas for what you might be able to give away.

- When I owned my cap stores, an embroidery machine in-house enabled me to stitch custom hats, shirts, etc. I used to offer a free custom embroidered cap to anyone that owned a business so that they could see the quality of our work. We gave away a lot of free caps, but we also picked up a lot of new business.

- I know a woman that helps people make better decisions about hiring a new employee. She does this by using an assessment that provides the employer with great information about a potential employee. She will offer one free assessment so people can see how the power of the information she provides makes their decision easier.

- A gentleman I know offers the service of recovering overpaid taxes to the IRS. He provides people with a free analysis of their past three years of income tax returns. If he finds any overpaid taxes, he receives a percentage of the refund. If he doesn't find anything, he gets nothing. It's a risk for him, but it normally works out very well.

Many of you might be thinking that these examples work fine if you have a business that provides a tangible result such as a hat or an assessment or a large check. But what happens if your business sells only an intangible? Check out these cool examples.

- An insurance agent offers a free lunch at a very nice restaurant to people that want to discuss their financial needs. By having lunch with them, she gets to start building a relationship with people, and she closes lots of new business.

- A Realtor® I know offers people a free neighborhood analysis. Many times, people want to know what's going on in their neighborhood or what the selling price is of homes down the street. She provides them this information at no cost because she knows that they will talk to her first when it comes to selling their current home and purchasing their new home.

As you can see, FREE can help just about anybody grab the attention of their listeners. Start finding a way to incorporate this powerful word into your elevator speech and watch how people will react.

✔ **Action Plan:**

From this day forth, I will work to see how I can offer something of value for free because giving away something that has true value will always help grab the attention of my listeners and entice people to start doing business with me.

Always end on a high note.

Q. How important is it that I have some sort of slogan or tag line for my elevator speech?

Many people end their elevator speech with something like, "Call me," or "I have cards and brochures in the back of the room." Every time I hear this, I watch to see if anyone actually rushes to the back of the room to pick up one of their cards or brochures or struggles to pull out their cell phone to call the person.

I believe that every good elevator speech should end with some sort of tag line or slogan about your company. This memorable closing not only helps people remember you, but also helps you stand out from the crowd. Here are a few examples from some friends of mine.

- I'm the Rose in the field of insurance

- A plethora of perfect promotional products

- You don't need no teeth to eat our meat

- Friends don't let friends drive dirty cars

Every time people hear your tag line, they will immediately think of you. Look at some of the biggest companies in the world. Try to remember some of the tag lines that they have used. Think about Pepsi, Coke, McDonald's, Burger King, and others. They all have tag lines that I am sure you can remember at a moment's notice. You must try to come up with something at the end of your commercial, some sort of phrase, some sort of tag line, that is going to make people remember your company when they hear those words. Come up with a great tag line, and people will always remember you.

✔**Action Plan:**

From this day forth, I will include some type of catchy or memorable phrase or tag line with my introduction so people will have a better chance to remember me.

Section Three

35th Flr.

How you say it makes all the difference.

Q. How much time should someone spend practicing the delivery of his or her elevator speech?

I have had the opportunity to help people put together some great elevator speeches. We have worked long and hard to come up with a fabulous message that is catchy, engaging, and really does the job their commercial is meant to do. Then, as I'm sitting in the audience waiting to hear our new creation delivered for the first time, I'm crushed when I see this great elevator speech delivered with so little enthusiasm and so little attitude that it just falls completely flat and has no major impact on the people hearing it.

Make sure that you have passion, excitement, and enthusiasm when you present your elevator speech. There is an old line that says something like, "If you can't get excited about your message, how can you expect anyone else to either?" Tom Peters says, "Forget all the conventional 'rules' but one. There is one golden rule: Stick to topics you deeply care about, and do not keep your passion buttoned inside your vest. An audiences' biggest turn on is the speaker's obvious enthusiasm. If you are lukewarm about the issue, forget it!"

So, to answer your question about how long you should practice the delivery of your introduction, my answer is as long as it takes to feel comfortable with the material and until you develop the proper level of passion, excitement, and attitude that will show your audience just how much you believe in your message. For some people, that might be a lifetime of practicing. However, if you are speaking from the heart and you have true passion for your message, you're practice time will be relatively short.

✔ Action Plan:

From this day forth, I will be excited, enthusiastic, and passionate about my elevator speech, because these things are contagious, and if I can't get excited about my business, how can I expect other people to get excited?

Be careful of your verbal speed.

Q. When I get very nervous, I tend to start speaking very fast. How can I fix that?

Fast speech is like fine print. It's easy to ignore. Radio and television commercials sometimes rely on this technique. At the end of an otherwise great offer, you hear an announcer running through a list of restrictions and qualifications that water down the offer. During this segment of the commercial, the announcer speaks so fast you can barely understand the message. Listeners tune out if speakers don't make listening comfortable. It's the speaker's job to make it easy and comfortable for the audience to listen.

If you habitually talk fast, you need a variety of ways to punctuate your speech. The most natural punctuation for speech is the pause you take when you reach for a breath. Speech, without the punctuation of pauses, is unclear and hard to listen to. It makes listeners uncomfortable, not just because of the speed itself. The unrelenting stream of sound never gives us a chance to rest and ponder the movement of the speaker's thought.

Here are a few ways to help slow down your speaking.

- Look people in the eye when you are speaking. That will slow you down, because you get feedback from your listener. You can see whether or not your listener understands what you are saying. That sense of connection with your target will help you pace your words.

- Breathe more often. You will have more energy for your voice, and you will feel calmer. You will have enough air to keep the energy in your voice right through to the end of the phrase.

- Pause between your phrases. The pauses will give your listeners a chance to absorb what you've said. Speech that comes from a person who is breathing deeply and regularly is easier to hear and understand.

Slowing down is a question of punctuation. Make sure you punctuate your speech by controlling and varying your pace, using focused pauses, and taking more frequent breaths. You'll not only hold the attention of your audience, you'll also deliver your points more powerfully and persuasively. (Thank you ECG Inc. for this valuable information.)

✔ Action Plan:

From this day forth, I will know my elevator speech inside and out so when I present it to people, I'll be able to say it in a relaxed manner and not feel like I'm rushing through it.

The simplest things are the easiest to forget.

Q. Are there certain things you never want to forget when you are delivering your elevator speech?

Here is one thing that you should never, ever forget when speaking with others. You need to remember to breathe. As simple as that sounds, there are many times people will just ramble on, tossing out one random thought after another. After a while, they start to become tense and stressed and uncomfortable. Are they having a nervous breakdown? No, they just forgot to breathe.

You can speak only as well as you breathe. Control your breath, and you begin to control your speaking voice. Also, better breathing reduces tension in the neck and shoulders that can inhibit your best natural voice. Always remember that your voice is a great wind instrument. Where does this wind come from? Keep reading.

The muscles between the ribs contract when you take a breath, and the ribs swing up and out. The diaphragm contracts, then descends and flattens, causing a slight displacement of abdominal organs and an expansion of the upper end of the abdomen. The size of the chest cavity increases, and air rushes in to fill the vacuum. When you exhale, muscles relax and return to the resting position, and air is forced out of the lungs. One of the best ways to help this process is by standing in a comfortable position, not rigidly straight or slumped over. (Thank you MIT for this valuable information.)

If you want to be able to deliver your elevator speech the way it was meant to be delivered, remember always to take it slow and breathe, because the more you breathe, the better your delivery will be.

✔ **Action Plan:**

From this day forth, I will always remember to breathe while I'm delivering my elevator speech to others so I will feel more physically comfortable when talking to people.

Speak up and be heard.

Q. When I deliver my thirty-second commercial at a networking event, I always hate using the microphone. I don't know why, but I just do. Any thoughts about this?

If you don't like using the microphone, I suggest you don't use it. Of course, most people won't hear what you are saying, and that makes it very difficult to create a connection with you.

There are few things that can kill a great elevator speech more than not being able to hear what is said. If you think people will strain to hear every word you say, you are kidding yourself. People will listen for a few seconds and then stop trying to listen.

Here are a few tips to make sure people hear you.

- Speak at a volume and at a level of clarity at which everybody will understand what you are saying.

- Watch the people that speak before you so you know the proper way to use the microphone.

- Hold the microphone up close to your mouth for the best results.

- Try to know the power of your voice. If you speak softly, make the most of the microphone. If you speak loudly, go easy on the microphone, so you don't deafen your audience.

- If the person in front of you decided not to use the microphone, that doesn't mean you shouldn't use it yourself. If it will help people hear you, USE IT!!

One last piece of advice for you: If you really freak out when you have to use a microphone, I would suggest you check out a chapter of Toastmasters. They will teach you how to speak and how to use the proper volume, and they will help you focus on your clarity.

✔ Action Plan I:

From this day forth, I will start to feel more comfortable using a microphone because I know that the better people can hear me, the better chance there is of creating a connection.

✔ Action Plan II:

From this day forth, I will use the best techniques possible when I use a microphone so my elevator speech is clear and easy for everyone to understand.

Practice really does make perfect.

Q. Every time I try to deliver my elevator speech, whether to a group or to an individual, I always get nervous, and I forget what I had planned on saying. WHAT'S WRONG WITH ME??

In my first book, *50 Top Tips, a Simple Guide to Networking Success*, I stated that if people want to be successful networkers, they must start attending lots of connection functions. The more functions they attend, the more comfortable they become. The more comfortable they become, the more success they will enjoy.

In regard to your elevator speech, the same rule holds true. If you want to feel more comfortable when you deliver your elevator speech, you need to go out and start using it EVERY SINGLE DAY!! I offer a program that helps people develop killer thirty-second introductions. All modesty aside, I've come up with some amazing elevator speeches. However, I'll listen to the people that I've worked with deliver their carefully crafted speech, and they will BUTCHER the message we spent so much time working on together.

To have a powerful, effective, and successful elevator speech, you need to go out and practice it the very first day you create it. If not, it will become too uncomfortable for you to use and you'll regress back to your old, ineffective way of answering the question, "What do you do?"

Remember that old line, "Practice makes perfect?" Well, I am an avid golfer. I know that when I go out and practice, my game is better. Every so often, I'll call my favorite pro and get a lesson or two. Unless I immediately start using the new ideas that he taught me, I have totally wasted my money. I can only get better by working with the new things I was taught.

The idea of practice is so important and so vital to life that the Dalai Lama even wrote a book called *How to Practice*. Here is a brief description of the book.

"*How to Practice* will guide you toward opening your heart, refraining from doing harm, maintaining mental tranquility, and more. The Dalai Lama shows us how to overcome our everyday obstacles, from feelings of anger and mistrust to jealousy, insecurity, and counterproductive thinking. Imbued with His Holiness's vivacious spirit and sense of playfulness, *How to Practice* offers the Dalai Lama's own sage and very practical insight into the human psyche and what binds us all together."

I can't say if practicing your elevator speech will open your heart or provide insight into the human psyche. However, I can say that the more you practice it, the more tweaking you can do to it, and the more success you will have with it.

✔ Action Plan:

From this day forth, I will practice my elevator speech on a regular basis until I become comfortable using it at any function or event.

Overcome the number one fear of creating connections.

Q. I have been working on my elevator speech for quite some time, and I feel I have a good one. The problem I face is that I'm still nervous about approaching new people. Any suggestions?

You are in good company. Approaching new people is the number one fear people experience when they meet and connect with new people. Here are a few ideas that will make approaching new people a bit easier for you.

- The first thing to understand is that almost everyone experiences this fear at one time or another. Yes, even I, Dave Sherman, sometimes have to deal with the fear of approaching new people. It is normal to feel a bit nervous when you are about to approach complete strangers and attempt to start a conversation with them. By embracing the concept that you aren't the ONLY one in the room that feels nervous, you should start to feel a little better.

- Start to believe that many people will be GRATEFUL that you approached them and began a conversation with them. If you see people standing by themselves, one of the greatest gifts you can give them is to walk up to them, introduce yourself, and start talking about ANYTHING!! Ever notice how much more comfortable you feel at an event when you are engaged in conversation with others? Have you noticed that once you start talking to one person, other people are more likely to approach you and start talking to you? The sooner you begin to chat with people at a function, the faster you will begin to relax, and you will begin to look more confident and self assured in the eyes of others.

■ If, by some freak chance, the people you introduce yourself to don't seem very warm or friendly, DON'T INTERNALIZE IT!! You have done absolutely nothing wrong. The biggest mistake you can make while networking is to think that you have done something wrong if other people don't respond to you in the way you expected them to. You have no idea what these people are going through. You don't know if they are having a bad day, not feeling well, or maybe dealing with a serious personal issue. It's also possible that some of the people you meet might just be JERKS!! If you approach people with the honest intention of meeting them to learn who they are and how you might be able to help them, you can hardly ever be wrong.

These three ideas should help you when it comes to meeting lots of new and exciting people at your next connection event. However, you need to make the decision that you are going to start using one of these tips. If not, you'll never meet the amount of people you need to meet to grow your business and enhance your life.

✔ Action Plan:

From this day forth, I will ALWAYS remember that everyone is somewhat nervous when it comes to meeting and connecting with others, and I will use this little known fact to help make me more fearless and to make other people fearless, too.

41st Flr.

Overcome a few more fears in your life.

Q. I still need a bit more help. Any other suggestions on how to be more comfortable and confident with creating connections?

In all the years I have been inspiring people to become better and more comfortable when connecting with others, I have discovered that the number one reason why people don't create these valuable connections is FEAR! More than ninety percent of people who network have some level of fear. The amazing part is that some of the people don't look like the type of person who would be nervous.

I would like to offer two simple tips on how to feel more comfortable when connecting with others. If you embrace this information, you will become more comfortable while networking, and you will help others become more comfortable, too.

TIP # 1. The best way to start feeling more comfortable talking to new people is to go out and start talking to people EVERYWHERE!! When I say everywhere, I mean everywhere. I'm talking grocery store lines, bank lines, lines waiting to board an airplane, groups inside elevators, and anywhere else. It isn't difficult to do. All you need to do is make a friendly comment about almost anything. In an elevator, ask how the person's day is going. In an airplane line, make light of the lengthy security process you just went through. By talking to strangers, you are giving them permission to do the same with you. What you say doesn't really matter. What matters is that by practicing talking to anyone, not only are you helping yourself feel more comfortable, but you are making the other person feel more comfortable, too.

I also suggest that you start carrying on conversations with what I like to call non-threatening individuals. Some examples would be your UPS person, your bank teller, your next-door neighbor. I used to use your postal carrier as an example of a non-threatening individual, but over the past few years, some of them have become a bit more threatening than others. Still, most postal people are very kind, very peaceful people. The reason these people are so easy to talk with is that they no impact on the success or failure of your life. With these people, you can have easy comfortable conversations, and the experience gives you the opportunity to practice talking with people in general.

TIP #2. If you need a little extra push to get started, I want to suggest that you motivate yourself into being a great networker. Think about the last time that you had to really pump yourself up to do something. It might have been a difficult golf shot, or a presentation to an important client, or a first date with that special girl. You said things to yourself like, "Yes, I can do this." "I know I'm going to do well at this." "I will succeed." It's the same thing in networking. As you walk into a function, say to yourself, "OK, I'm going to go in here; I'm going to meet people. I'm going see how I can help these individuals. I'm going to do this; I can do this," and keep saying this to yourself. Say, "I can do this, I can do this, I can do this."

Brian Tracy once said, "Fake it until you make it," because by convincing yourself that you are a great connector, the better connector you will be. Just keep saying to yourself, "I'm a fearless connector; I'm a fearless connector." Get yourself pumped up and ready to go, and you'll see just how fearless you can really be.

✔ **Action Plan I:**

From this day forth, I will start talking to people wherever I might be because it will make me feel better, and it will make the other people fell better as well.

✔ **Action Plan II:**

From this day forth, I will pump myself up on a regular basis and convince myself each day that I am a fearless connector until the day comes that I actually am I fearless connector.

Always keep a smile on your face.

Q. After I tell people my elevator speech, what can I do to increase the number of people that continue the conversation I started?

An elevator speech is meant to grab people's attention, engage people in conversation about your business and encourage them to say, "TELL ME MORE!" However, after you have said your introduction, one of the simplest and easiest ways to deepen the connection you just created is with a smile.

Smiles are one of the most powerful facial expressions you can share when you meet another human being. Smiles make you more approachable, they make you appear warmer, and they make you appear friendlier. Some people even think that smiles make people look more intelligent. If that were the case, I'd have plastic surgery to have a smile permanently plastered on my face.

Smiles also make other people feel more comfortable. If you are at a connection event and you decide that you want to approach a few people and make some introductions, are you going to walk up to that guy with the scowl on his face? NO WAY!! You are going to look for the friendliest people you can find, and they are the ones with a smile on their face.

Here are a few other reasons why a great smile is so important to meeting people.

1) Smiles show friendship. They are kind of like a peace offering for the new people you are meeting. Smiles show them that you are friendly and warm and have a desire to meet them.

2) Smiles make new friends. They are a universally recognized symbol of kindness. All over the world, the smile is used to create the beginning of many relationships.

3) Smiles make other people's day brighter. Think about the people you know that always have a smile on their face. We typically feel happier when we see them.

4) Smiles improve your day. Try this little experiment. The next time you are having a bad day, unclench your jaws for a while and smile. I guarantee that you will start to feel much better.

5) Smiles look better than a frown. This idea is obvious, but to prove my point, walk around your office or take a look around the next restaurant you visit, and see how much better a smile looks instead of a frown.

6) Smiles put others at ease. When meeting people for the first time, the best way to create connections is to do what you can to help make the other people feel more comfortable.

7) Smiles are *always* enjoyable to give and receive. Plain and simple, smiling just makes us feel good, and it will always make others feel good, too.

8) Smiles leave favorable impressions. As you know, you only have one chance to make a great first impression. A smile will help you make this possible.

9) Smiles make you look happy, confident, and self-assured. People want to be associated with people who

are happy, confident, and self-assured. Smile more often, and people will want to meet you.

10) Smiles can be the start of a lifetime relationship. Ahh, the best one for last! All great relationships must have a starting point. In most cases, that starting point is a great smile.

If you want to meet more people, make more connections, be more successful, and enjoy a happier and healthier life overall, wipe that scowl off of your face and start smiling more. You will look better, feel better, and best of all, people will start warming up to you more often and more quickly.

✔ Action Plan:

From this day forth, I will remember the power of a nice smile, and I will keep one on my face whenever possible because it will make me more approachable, more comfortable, and maybe even more intelligent.

Every good introduction starts with a good handshake.

Q. I heard you speak once about the importance of a good handshake. How can your handshake help with your elevator speech?

When you meet someone for the first time, before you can launch into your elevator speech, you first have to make a formal introduction. One of the biggest parts of this introduction is the handshake. A good handshake can initiate a great connection.

Shaking hands is probably the most common gesture people use on a daily basis. Men and women alike use it constantly in business and social situations. It is typically the first contact between two people and the first chance to establish a connection and a relationship. Your handshake conveys an impressive, nonverbal message, many times before you speak verbally. It speaks loudly of your professionalism, confidence, trust- worthiness, and savvy. It is as common in America as it is around the world. In most countries, it is an accepted gesture of introduction, agreement, friendship, congratulation, and good-bye. With all that being true, have you ever given much thought to the form, style, or etiquette of your handshake?

Handshakes are very important to me. In January 1973, one month before my Bar Mitzvah (a ceremony that marks a Jewish boy's entry to adulthood within the Jewish community), my father sat me down and formally explained the proper way to shake hands. I still remember that precious moment with my dad like it was yesterday. Unfortunately, my father passed away five short years later, but his hand-shaking lesson lives on in me. My handshake has become one of the most recognizable aspects of my personality, so much so that it thoroughly impressed my future father-in law when I met him.

Many times our handshake forms the first impression ... an impression that speaks very loudly about who and what we are. What is your handshake saying about you?

Here are ten tips to help you ensure a powerful and confi-dent handshake in business.

1. Always stand up. Whether you are a man or a woman, you should rise.

2. Face the person squarely, not at an angle.

3. The handshake should be a "web to web" contact between your thumb and index finger. By shaking hands web to web, you avoid the dead fish or fingertip only handshake.

4. Thumbs should be straight up. Avoid rolling one hand over or under, for this may denote a power struggle.

5. Make direct eye contact, and hold the gaze through the introduction.

6. Smile, using a pleasant and approachable smile, not an overly big grin.

7. Carry papers, briefcase, drinks, etc., in the left hand leaving the right hand free for shaking hands.

8. Do not squeeze someone's hand too hard (bone crush-ing) or too soft (dead fish); these are both signs of insecurity.

9. Avoid pumping the hand up and down excessively.

10. The person who is being introduced "to," should extend his or her hand first.

(Thank you to Cynthia Grasso from the Charleston School of Protocol)

Here's one last piece of information for you. I am often asked what to do if you get the dead fish or incorrect handshake. Should you correct it? NO! Absolutely not! The number one rule of etiquette is to let the other person save face. Do not embarrass anyone at any cost, even if it causes you to shake hands incorrectly (for example, by reaching across a desk or object). Although you know the technique is incorrect, avoid embarrassing the other person. Embarrassment would not add positively to the building of a relationship, the result if you begin by correcting them. More importantly, if people give you a dead fish handshake, it is due to one of two things: They were never taught the correct way to shake someone's hand, or they are uncertain. (In business, neither is viewed positively.) Either way, it is at this point that we start to read the other person and truly begin to communicate.

Your handshake is a very important part of who you are. Once you understand and implement the correct etiquette, your handshake will help your introduction. I teach people to think of their handshake as their signature. Use it as a tool to speak about yourself in a positive and powerful way.

✔ Action Plan:

From this day forth, I will make sure my handshake is sending the right impression to the people I meet, because I want to make the best of our first physical contact.

44th Flr.

Remember to look them in the eye.

Q. When I talk to people for a period of time, I always feel I'm staring at them too much. How can I keep good eye contact without freaking the other person out?

If you meet many people in your daily life, it's a good idea to think about how you make eye contact. It is, after all, one of the first signs people use to form an impression of you! If you spend time observing people, you will soon recognize that there are many different eye contact styles.

■ **The Fixed-Stare Style:**

Their eyes never leave you and practically bore through you. Occasionally, this style is used as a power trick to intimidate or to give the impression that people are more confident than they really are. This style has been used by politicians who have been thoroughly coached on how to appear a lot more trustworthy than they often turn out to be!

■ **The Darting-Glance Style:**

They do look at you—but with very brief glances. They tend to look at you only when your gaze is averted. This style can give the impression of either low self-confidence or lack of trustworthiness, so if it happens to be your natural style, you may wish to remedy the situation rather than transmit such a nonverbal message.

■ **The No-Eye-Contact Style:**

Their eyes rarely, if ever, meet yours. They use peripheral vision to watch you. This style is much favored by country dwellers whose lifestyle has not included many opportunities for gazing into the eyes of other humans.

You may have noticed, while out in the open country, that there is a tendency to use somewhat less eye contact and to stand farther from one another than would be the norm on a city street. As with the Darting Glance, this style can be misinterpreted; however, the No-Eye-Contact style is more likely to be a learned behavior than an essential part of their thinking strategy.

■ **The Turn-And-Turn-About Style:**

This is the most common style. They look quite steadily at you while you are speaking. However, if you appear to find this uncomfortable, they will look away occasionally to avoid creating tension. When it is your turn to speak, you look at them steadily while they still meet your gaze but look away a little more (to think, gather thoughts, check feelings, etc.).

To make more connections with others, here are a few ways to deal with the above mentioned styles.

■ **If they use the Fixed Stare:**

While speaking to them, look at them for longer than you might otherwise do. However, avoid getting into I-will-not-look-away-until-you-do competition. When you are doing the listening, give them quite sustained eye contact. (If, at first, you find this a little uncomfortable, you can ease your own tension by varying your expression and by using head nods and "uh-huh" sounds.)

- **If they use Darting Glances:**

  Giving them sustained eye contact will be perceived as aggressive or even intimidating. Adopt a somewhat similar style by looking away more than might be normal for you, especially when you are doing the speaking.

- **If they use minimal eye contact:**

  Make much less eye contact than you might normally do. Also, try practicing using peripheral vision to watch them.

(Thank you, Pegasus NLP, for some of this information)

As you can see, good eye contact is very important in making more connections with others. However, it takes a lot of practice to feel comfortable with it. So, the next time you're talking to people, think about how your eyes can tell so much about who you are.

Speak Your Speech Before You Write your Speech.

Q. I'm ready to really start working on my elevator speech. What's the best way to write one?

One of the very first things I learned when I went into the speaking business was that it's a lot easier to write a spoken speech than it is to speak a written speech. Allow me to repeat that so you'll understand what I'm saying. When it comes to putting together a thirty-second commercial, it's much simpler to write down what you are saying than to try writing down random thoughts in order to make a speech out of them. Not only is it simpler, it makes your elevator speech more natural, more emotional, and more you. If you try to present an elevator speech that you wrote without speaking it yourself, it could come across as a bit stiff and less warm. It could be more difficult for you to present.

One of the greatest compliments I receive about my books is that they are so conversational. I have to admit to you that they are this way because I speak every word I want to include in the book before I write it. This way, you can get that feeling that you are really talking to me and not just reading a book.

If this concept is hard for you to grasp, don't stress about it. If the only thing you take from this section is that you need to write down your elevator speech before you present, you will be way ahead of the game. Many people never take the time to write down their thoughts, and they wonder why they forget to say certain things. If you spend a few moments and recite your introduction to yourself as you write it down, you'll start seeing much greater responses from your listeners.

✔ **Action Plan:**

From this day forth, I will always make the time to write down my elevator speech before I present it, and I will try to write the spoken word instead of speaking the written word.

One to One Elevator Speech Consulting With Dave Sherman

How can this program help you?

One of the most frequently asked questions at a networking event are "What do you do?" Unfortunately, most people don't have a great answer to this simple question. You will learn the steps necessary to create a powerful message that will not only tell people what they do but why they should be doing more business with you.

You will learn:

- Why the way you're currently answering the question, "What do you do?" is hurting your business

- What every elevator speech must contain to be successful

- How to create a new title for yourself that is more intriguing and more fun to use

- How to be more comfortable and confident when delivering your elevator speech

- And SO MUCH MORE

For only $295

Includes a one to two hour teleconference with Dave and unlimited e-mail follow-up.

For more information, please call Dave at 480-860-6100 or e-mail him at Dave@ConnectionPros.com

About the Author

Dave Sherman, a Professional Icebreaker, has been helping people all over the country create deep, powerful and productive connections with others that have helped them personally and professionally. Dave believes connections are not created by handing out your business card and telling people everything they NEVER wanted to know about your business. It's the process of creating a level of likeability and commonality with the people you meet. The more people you create this common bond with, the faster your business grows and the easier your life becomes.

As the founder and creator of "Connection Pros", a speaking, training, and consulting organization, Dave inspires people to look at the process of creating connections in a whole new light that is more effective, more comfortable, and more profitable. Dave is also the author of the best selling book, *50 TOP TIPS, A Simple Guide to Networking Success, Breaking the Ice—306 Great Conversation Starters* as well as numerous other CD and video programs.

Dave has had the pleasure of working with Wells Fargo, Southwest Airlines, Merrill Lynch, Smith Barney, American Express, Northwestern Mutual, Medtronic, and over a dozen Chambers of Commerce all over the country.

Dave has been married to Randi since 1988 and is the father to Lyndsi and Mathew and lives in beautiful Scottsdale, AZ. He loves golf, international travel, action movies and his only real vices these days are a glass of chardonnay and good Cuban cigar.

You can contact Dave at:

10128 N. 119th Place
Scottsdale, AZ 85259
480-860-6100-office
480-451-9484 – fax
Dave@ConnectionPros.com—email
www.ConnectionPros.com—website

Check Out Dave's Other Products

Books

Audio CDs

Video CDs

Check Here		Format	Price
❏	*50 Top Tips*	Book	$19.95
❏	*Breaking the Ice*	Book	$12.95
❏	**Both books (save almost $13.00)**		$20.00
❏	*Let's Get Ready to Network*	One Audio CD	$19.95
❏	*50 Top Tips*	Two Audio CDs	$39.95
❏	**Both programs (save almost $20.00)**		$40.00
❏	*The Most Important 10 Seconds*	One video Cd	$39.95
❏	*Seven Simple Steps*	One video CD	$39.95
❏	**Both programs (save almost $30.00)**		$50.00
❏	**Ultimate Success Pack (save almost $73.00)** Includes one of every product on this page		$99.00
		Total	$

Name_____Phone_____

Address_____

_____

E-mail address_____

Credit Card #_____EXP_____

Security Code (Three numbers on the back of your card)_____

Return to: Connection Pros
10128 N. 119th Place
Scottsdale, AZ 85259
Phone orders – 480-860-6100
Fax orders – 480-451-9484
Website orders – www.ConnectionPros.com